ALL ABOUT ARACHNIDS
WATER SPIDERS

by Natalie Deniston

pogo

Ideas for Parents and Teachers

Pogo Books let children practice reading informational text while introducing them to nonfiction features such as headings, labels, sidebars, maps, and diagrams, as well as a table of contents, glossary, and index.

Carefully leveled text with a strong photo match offers early fluent readers the support they need to succeed.

Before Reading

- "Walk" through the book and point out the various nonfiction features. Ask the student what purpose each feature serves.
- Look at the glossary together. Read and discuss the words.

Read the Book

- Have the child read the book independently.
- Invite them to list questions that arise from reading.

After Reading

- Discuss the child's questions. Talk about how they might find answers to those questions.
- Prompt the child to think more. Ask: Did you know about water spiders before reading this book? What more would you like to learn about them?

Pogo Books are published by Jump!
5357 Penn Avenue South
Minneapolis, MN 55419
www.jumplibrary.com

Copyright © 2025 Jump!
International copyright reserved in all countries. No part of this book may be reproduced in any form without written permission from the publisher.

Library of Congress Cataloging-in-Publication Data is available at www.loc.gov or upon request from the publisher.

ISBN: 979-8-89213-627-3 (hardcover)
ISBN: 979-8-89213-628-0 (paperback)
ISBN: 979-8-89213-629-7 (ebook)

Editor: Katie Chanez
Designer: Emma Almgren-Bersie

Photo Credits: blickwinkel/Alamy, cover, 8-9, 10, 12-13, 17, 18-19, 20-21; S_Chum/iStock, 1; Nature Picture Library/Alamy, 3, 6-7; Holger Kirk/Shutterstock, 4, 11, 23; Pavel Krasensky/Shutterstock, 5; Oxford Scientific/Getty, 14-15; Norbert Schuller/Wikimedia, 16.

Printed in the United States of America at Corporate Graphics in North Mankato, Minnesota.

TABLE OF CONTENTS

CHAPTER 1
Underwater Spiders 4

CHAPTER 2
On the Hunt 10

CHAPTER 3
Water Babies 16

ACTIVITIES & TOOLS
Try This! 22
Glossary 23
Index 24
To Learn More 24

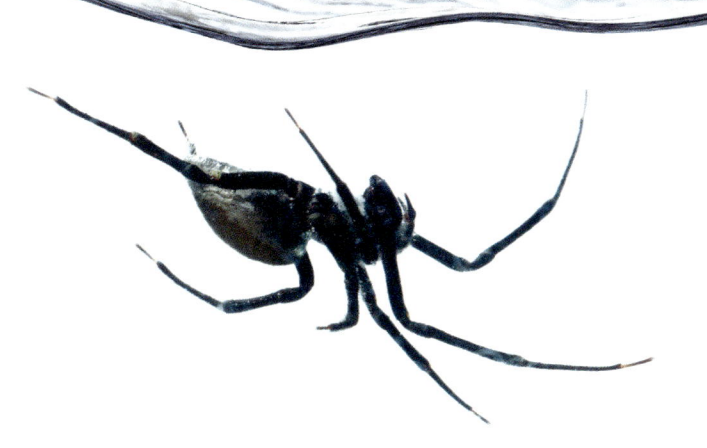

CHAPTER 1
UNDERWATER SPIDERS

A spider crawls on a plant. It is underwater! An air bubble is on the spider's back.

air bubble

Water spiders are the only **arachnids** that spend their entire lives underwater.

CHAPTER 1   5

How does a water spider breathe? It swims or crawls to the surface. It sticks its body out of the water. Air sticks to tiny hairs on the spider's abdomen. This creates an air bubble when the spider goes back underwater. The spider breathes air from the bubble.

6 CHAPTER 1

TAKE A LOOK!

What are the parts of a water spider? Take a look!

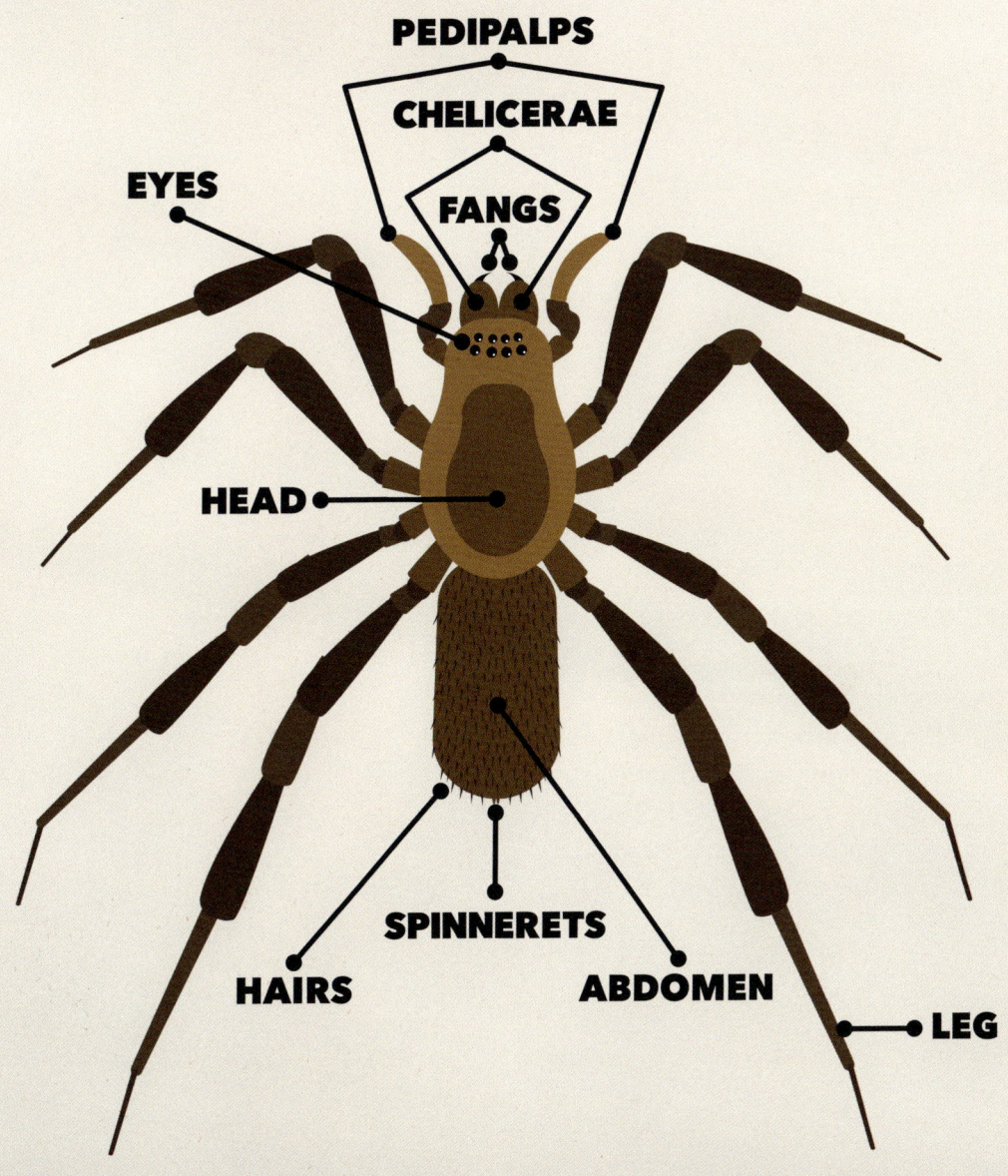

CHAPTER 1   7

Water spiders live in still or slow-moving water. This includes lakes, ponds, and streams. They make their homes near underwater plants. A spider spins a web between plants. The web holds air bubbles. The air bubbles combine to create a large bubble called a diving bell. This is a safe place for the spider to live and breathe.

DID YOU KNOW?

Water spiders are also called diving bell spiders. Diving bells are bell-shaped objects used to provide divers with air while underwater.

diving bell

CHAPTER 1   9

CHAPTER 2
ON THE HUNT

A water spider spends most of its time in its diving bell. About once a day, it goes to the surface for another air bubble. It brings it back to its bell.

Males swim outside the bell to hunt. One spots a small **crustacean**. He grabs it with his legs. He brings his **prey** to his bell to eat.

CHAPTER 2   11

Females often hunt from their bells. One waits for prey to swim by. An **insect** comes close. The spider pops out! She grabs the prey with her legs. She pulls it inside.

DID YOU KNOW?

A female builds a larger diving bell than a male. She has room for **mating** and for her **spiderlings**.

CHAPTER 2 13

All water spiders have strong jaws called chelicerae. A spider uses these to **inject** juices into its prey. The juices turn the prey's insides to liquid. The spider drinks it up!

CHAPTER 2

CHAPTER 3
WATER BABIES

A male water spider finds a female. He chases her. They swim together. Then they go into the female's bell. They mate.

The female lays 50 to 100 eggs. They go into a white egg sac made of silk. The female attaches it to her web. It stays in her bell. She guards it.

egg sac

After three to four weeks, spiderlings hatch. They live in the bell with mom for about one month. They grow and **molt**.

CHAPTER 3

After molting four times, the spiderlings leave the bell. They find spots to make their own bells.

DID YOU KNOW?

Some young water spiders fill empty shells with air. Why? The shells act as diving bells until the spiders can make their own webs!

CHAPTER 3

ACTIVITIES & TOOLS

TRY THIS!

MAKE YOUR OWN DIVING BELL

Make your own diving bell in this fun activity!

What You Need:
- 1 sheet of paper
- pencils, markers, or other drawing materials
- scissors
- 1 clear plastic cup
- clear tape
- container larger than the cup
- water

❶ Draw a spider on the piece of paper. Cut it out.

❷ Tape the spider to the inside of the cup.

❸ Fill the large container with water.

❹ Turn the cup upside down so the opening is facing the water. Slowly push it down into the water. How is the cup like a diving bell?

GLOSSARY

arachnids: Creatures with bodies divided into two parts, such as spiders or scorpions.

crustacean: A water creature that has an outer skeleton, such as a crab, lobster, or shrimp.

inject: To put something into a body through fangs.

insect: A small animal with three pairs of legs, one or two pairs of wings, and three main body parts.

mating: Coming together to produce babies.

molt: To shed an outer layer.

prey: Animals hunted by other animals for food.

spiderlings: Baby spiders.

INDEX

breathe 6, 8
bubble 4, 6, 8, 10
chelicerae 7, 14
crustacean 11
diving bell 8, 10, 11, 13, 16, 17, 19, 20
eggs 17
egg sac 17
hairs 6, 7
hatch 19
hunt 11, 13
inject 14
insect 13
mating 13, 16
molt 19, 20
plant 4, 8
prey 11, 13, 14
silk 17
spiderlings 13, 19, 20
underwater 4, 5, 6, 8
web 8, 17, 20

TO LEARN MORE

Finding more information is as easy as 1, 2, 3.

❶ Go to www.factsurfer.com
❷ Enter "waterspiders" into the search box.
❸ Choose your book to see a list of websites.